Disorientations: Groundings

Disorientations: Groundings

Jay Wright

Flood Editions, Chicago

Published by Flood Editions

www.floodeditions.com

ISBN 978-0-9838893-4-2

Cover illustration: Caravaggio,
St. Jerome Writing, c. 1605–1606.
Oil on canvas, 44 × 62 inches.
Courtesy of Galleria Borghese
Design and composition by Quemadura
Printed on acid-free, recycled paper
in the United States of America

This book was made possible in part through
a grant from the Illinois Arts Council

giri sọ̃

benne sọ̃

bọlọ sọ̃

sọ̃ dayi

giri sọ

Why does the Dane think his design
a complement to Being?

        Would Èṣù sustain him?
These bachelors sing a self-possession,
the perfect melodic orientation,
place and measure,
disfigured,

        a bell
tolling a pneumatic suffering.
Let me awaken a definition of suffering.
"Our task is not to penetrate into the essence of things."
Did I tell you I am learning a moon's ambition,
how to rope the pup into submission,
and teach the proper direction?
You will remember the discretion
Orion has taught its little suns;

            that leads
to a tuned ambivalence in every pulsing star.
All this dancing
becomes a measured probability,
a postulate of love's insistent

           imaginings.
Go away.

Become an ancestor, undone
by the grief you find in the bush.
Let the tales toll divinity,
or swell with the obscenity

                  of living.
Physics concerns only what we have learned to say.
I have a perfect cadence,
a lover and lady,

             a record
of what I have learned to sing.
I am neither Jew nor Greek.
What does that have to do with a Wednesday
in Bastrop, Texas,
where an atom chooses a summery frock
and goes calling from door

              to door?
There is an improbable gas in this desert,
one that might curry a new constellation,
and one ought to learn
how to distinguish between right and left.
Leave the gate open;
someone will appear in white garments
to measure the freestanding empiricism

                  of salvation,
and the sweetest motets will prepare
a labyrinth of apprehension.

             Don Alfonso
will improvise a descant for the water birch.

I speak as though the mechanics involved

had been decided,

as though our common syntax,

lacking the weight of inquiry,

had made our exchange efficiently honest,

a perfect symmetry binding a thought to its word.

This argues no struggle,

though I know there will be no way to measure my path,

or the probable constraint

that keeps me, insatiable, attuned to my element.

That might be love,

or a thirst for blood, or a first

ontological absolute amplified by a silence.

Speak now of the difficult eucalyptus,

the agapanthi,

the absolute density that has never appeared.

And I hear there will be a baptism on the Nile this afternoon,

stirring an Etruscan envy, a Roman insecurity.

I ask you now to consider the old poet
as he sits in his Bradford garden,
to embrace his Phaedo and to think
                of that sultry appearance,
an exuberant disappearance he might have invoked.
"In my solitude,"
I have become disobedient to Yoruba matters,
and all things concerning an abandonment,
a betrayal of death.
Don Lupe figured such discomfort,
yesterday,
at twilight,
in La Posada,
and struck that match-kempt arrogance
                peculiar to Santa Fe.
Think of faith,
if you must,
the responsible mind that lies athwart
the irresponsible notion of being,
and of that peculiar dispossession
that becomes a form of freedom.
                Was there a burial?
In these Prairie Provinces,
beaver structures an avocation

that will never lend itself to any deductive
abstraction, or ever get used to the hymnal
feel embodied in muskets, copper kettles,

                        fishhooks and brandy.
I say again
that one must learn to live a stringy existence,
and be capable of such boundless deviations
that you might forget your name,
or your purpose,
and go lightning quick through a keyhole
you take for the eye of God.
The old poet has done a study
of exploration, of rhythm as ethos,
that metrical surrogate
that speaks of borrowing and that troubled
and troubling relationship he has given
an ancient name.
I hear that one should take particular ease
in calculation and the economy embodied
in small forms,
the body that stands apart from itself,
turning geometrically through the algebra
                of its constructive presence.
Some will say the garden teaches these mistakes.
And who will discover the redemption
the ruby-throated hummingbird
offers in its interrupted
                        flight?

Some say the spirit does no work. All Greek
and spatial, I have set myself to prove
the intuitive descent that will move
love's thorough device. I might have spoken
with my face uncovered, with an oblique
unbidden swerve to a body broken
by grief, though I know only concealment,
the limit proposed by an astringent
rhyme, translation's promise, never mended.
I keep myself in September's logic,
in bees doing their fall work, suspended
in a narrative passage, iambic,
all magnitudes in proportion. I mark
my secular hymnal, the extended
derivation on display, authentic
silence that structures a voice in the dark.

Qué muerte tan larga llevan las flores en tu seno . . .
I would fasten myself to that rhythm,
an anniversary of salt and serenity,
if I were only sure the stars would close their wounds
and send me fleeing from ash.

                         Who is Molinari,
with his caked fingernails and an eye
for Delphic hemlock?
How would he know that his exuberant
singing in the year I was born

                         disturbs me now?
Flowers at this wake
should be claveles o rosas, guests,
wearing the night's frozen clothes.

I came into this valley,
looking for the space beyond God.
So the flowers will bear the eternal death,
my intangible form,

                         that Damascene irony
knocked up for Easter,
an insatiable double event.
Stratis Thalassinos declares himself disappointed,

repudiates my borrowing from the grave-endowed Egyptian,
calls upon the Cusan
to establish an ordinal intention
                    in my morning office,
and accuses me of being in disguise.

I cannot argue the infinite unfolding
                    at sea in this valley,
                        or the redemptive necessity
                            when the singing fades.

The biblical Baca loves to betray me by measuring
the water in this room in Buenos Aires.
            Qué bromazo tan grande . . .
He parades his landscape—
            five floors up on a corner at Las Heras,
            a window above Charcas y Maipú,
            un zaguán in Calle Arcos,
            a garden in the Plaza Italia,
a Mali awakening structured at La Recoleta.

Molinari will defend me.
He, after all, standing in a "florid summer,"
has seen a blue horse and a transparent bull.
Could he have traveled with the librarian
along the Calle Florida,
improvising sombras and inscriptions, a hostage
to poppies and his own death, married perhaps

to a river's edge and saffron?
I would ask him to read the city's book,
the disinherited sadness,
that extensive proportion
                              quickly buried.

Baca has me in his eye; he distrusts me.
He would like to be that indigenous third,
a master of odes that have traveled blind.
All that Baca endures
Molinari approves in his speechless wind
and bodiless rivers, in the desecration
                              of sacred grain,
in the larga tristeza desterrada,
embodied in an imperfect cadence,
these odes that speak of the momentary,
changeable form of a death on the River Plate.
No pienso nada más que en ti:
        the incantatory capacity of silence.

The friendly little immigrant will speak to me,
insisting upon its place within my body.
You might ask how the grave could treat such a shoddy
assignation, and go scouting a pedigree
or fall fearfully attuned to a binary

moment, that benevolent colloquy, oddly
exact, a density the deed will embody,
a star birth testing its own security.

Doña Fiel knows death's prosody, and knows the tau
of its bones, feels the rush in impermanence;
these virtues feed our intuition, give offense.

I was once in Banderilla, and took a vow
the akusmata extolled for its perfect sense;
they loved my presence, and await me even now.

Cursus Ensemble

A

Our dust and meter fall
in campo aperto, logical
        field without substance.

B

That first electric composition,
which comes as night,
        remains
        God's only constancy.

C

If the voice chants a stellar
contingency,
        would that pulse be
        ultimately stable?

D

Let the flow go
where the body becomes
                immeasurable,
                broken by its solace.

E

Such a perceptive entanglement,
beyond crucifixion,
gives
        wings to our rhythm.

F

Will datura thread an impure state,
sing chronon's song,
fix a
        word without a body?

G

Impertinent clausula will skirr
this effusion,
music's
        anima animus.

An Irish November carries its own tune.
Transported logic phrases an offense.
Here, in an air that dare not challenge a kiva choir,
those from a frangible coast
see themselves with a ghost
of a chance to spell heartache,
and reap an angel's capacity for heartbreak.
One could no more turn foresters upon these dense
urban streets. Tell me now if one could aspire
to string an April Provençal never as immune
as a lover with a stake
in self-deception, with an opaque
regard for love's rainy and northernmost
limits. Appoint such a one November's provost.

My sister has traced my absence, an arc
derelict and gravitational. I
mean to restore my shadowy orbit
to confound the Dane, with his double spark

and little suns all set to a limit.
The Cusan knows nothing will satisfy
such an indeterminate relation.
I suppose myself unaccountable,

a slight event, figured transformation,
breaking bonds, proposing nothing stable.
This dactyl remains indisputable.

Out of the salt-box, up the river on a barge,
Lucy s'incline.
What does it mean
when the Québécois lose their large
ambition? I declare myself confused,
a late romancer consummately abused
by governors and garbage men. Is it my fate
to remain unfettered and state-
less, while my lady wears me like a glove?
What would this peasant do for love?
Oh, I would be no eccentric bird,
perched on the water, therefore
lost to the curious eye, but a tenor
with a gift for the healing third.

There is a derelict intention in love,
a chronic fabulation that never sits right.
One, two, or three might be the hour of regress.
Oh, there waits nothing like the distress
such plucked berries reprove;
they get under the skin, read Petrarch through Donne,
all dunable relations too much in hand.
Peter just has found a clever form. Might
his betrayal open sunsets to dawn,
spawn whatever conspiracy
two who have met on a bland
winter evening enflame? How artful
that appears, delinquent and delightful,
a thorough response to a lunacy.

Quatre études de rythme

1

Tres hermanicas eran—tres hermanicas son.
Two well exposed to failure, one who had lost the tone.
Nothing comes alive with this; green is a marrow bone.
Morenica y sabrosica, away with el varón.
Granada courts Perico; a Francia lo mandó.
All for the best in Gádir, a nadar se echó.
Discounting lime and red stone, who would ask for more?
Not for the father sleeping, not for the angel's core.

2

These are the elements fit for a wedding,
        fecha, rica e auondada.
We shall take a moment to compose this garden.
        My village abandoned
its dasiri, though everything remains in place,
        the antiquated
rock and wood present at the crossroads,
        pure and resuscitated.

3

¡Que alto pino es la memoria del amor!
The offensive poet would measure that once
expansive history,
                                    a seed perturbation,
given in a name's confusion.
Surely, it must hover and sift,
begin its decline, and find
its subjective force insufficient.

4

Suppose the papagayo green, a rueda
quinta y perfecta, transcribed as a turtle-dove
on a dry branch and every feast day born in debt.
                    Within this geometry,
the sun begins its cautious decline,
that passage into the earth's eye.
Praise that woman's radiance,
                                    always opposed to the light.

Gorostiza sings a radiant atmosphere,
splintered air, an unending fall; oh, how he cries
for a woman's slow tear, a subtle flame, austere
in its Sabbath habits. Could these be fertile lies?

Larache gives birth to a temperate sadness,
goes from cradle to cradle dispensing secret
names, promising widows in Córdoba, the stress
that justifies death's probabilities, and yet

the young will send for meat at the butcher's, for wine
from the fields, and call our attention to the green
banana trees along the wedding route, the spine,

lume spento, of a world marked by no design.
Who could love Gorostiza's soul, his wellspring dry,
his conjugal skill no more than a lullaby?

No one says water in Lagos.
That equation has been solved.
We sit with the ornamental molecule,
where all is danger, and every chemical bond
foretells a frozen

        ingenuity.

        You must forgive
this intrusion, you must forgive
God's imperfection.

        Such heavy water
courses through this song.
Now, think of the lovely density
that makes such a tale expansive.

Why must we always speak to the corantados,
find the east a blessing, or see the triple cross
as nothing at all? Each spirit shows dos lados,
a linear incertitude, that special gloss

and pertinent mask the calabash must display.
You must have heard that singer's sly dithyrambos,
and have seen, or felt, the lumen going astray.
Gorostiza fishes by moonlight, a pathos

Baca will not allow, even when the net's black threads
recover a two-fold night and the world withdraws.
Should we be free from delusion, the light that spreads

its withering strength in space? Nothing of the flaws
in impunity should concern us, not the rose
of ash, nor the trace that brings this field to a close.

Must all interludes be auspicious,
melodic inversions,
a celibate ascent from tonic to dominant,
leading to that fat cat five steps below?
You see the flaw
they call progression.

benne sọ

Somewhere between here and Belen,
the Rio Grande will narrow to a muddy bead,
no more than three feet across from shore to shore.
My friend, Nick Markulis, claims
he loves the river's color there, and will bathe
his toes in the water, and will go on and on
about a dry river in Athens that measures its life
                              in olive groves.
Stratis Thalassinos told me about these peculiar
waters that disappear and turn up again,
and, of course, you know of Arethusa's
fountain in Syracuse.
I do not accuse Markopoulos (do I have
the name right?—Markopoulos, Markulis,
fugitive names, fugitive lives docking in Halifax)
of being too conversant with asphodel meadows,
but one cannot remain composed
when hunters and cultic figures press their claims
upon a sainted afternoon.
Think now of the intimate authority of La Candelaria,
the Sunday morning concert,
the walk through the abandoned streets,

where all was an occasion of Bogotá,
a memory of Mazatlán, a shaping
necessity we might have met at Salamis.
Who can be sure
that this white cloth will be dissolved by death?

Arthurian Trio

1

There, by that river birch, a martyr's red
lies softly in the eye, a charity
decently composed, a triviality
the spirit will endure. No one will thread

an accidental life, or a rhythm bred
by a whispered promise, through that city.
We have awakened a civility
in a garden concerned with the dead.

Who are we to allow God to suffer,
and to offer to mend the world from our souls'
intrinsic darkness? There is a patience

in our appetite for loss, a rougher
density that impatiently consoles
a morning stirred by a body's coherence.

2

I now place this body in its modal box,
its bones opposed; I remember the orthodox
song the seed composed for its grainy clavicle.
Plotinus felt this secret rain, a particle
melody unfolding over the soul's terrain,
and proposed himself defined by a most urbane
and breathing sphere.
                        Let us take him at his word,
though the word displays a blemish, at once absurd
and dependable—all rest a perfect passage
through time, every microstate a new coinage.

The realized design will always sit in shadow;
a woven cotton band will address the shallow
sun at the crossroads, the changing magnetic field,
the possible planetary motion concealed
by the coherent self.
                        The evidence for such
energy depends upon a fault, or a touch
perturbative, expansive, indifferent to seed.
That would be music, a text the body would read,

given the darkness at its core. What could be more
constructive than an open book, a metaphor
without a living authority, aesthetic
misgivings? Think now of this page as ascetic,
changing in response to an unforgiving weight.

This hermetic Parisian thinks love an innate
conception, a first form without limit, and yet
he savors death's jeweled presence, an amulet
instructive in its being, troubled by desire.
Only an Arthurian mind could aspire
to this galactic cluster, disorder's syntax.
This prophet holds his peace, and overlooks his lax
attention to sacrifice and divinity.
Our Parisian believes in measureless conjury
and the parallax that measures all rampant souls.

On the rue des Ecoles a small hotel consoles
the poet steeped in May.
                              Nothing ever loses
its being; or so says Bruno, who refuses
God's transfiguration and the landscape implied
by the smallest seed, a linear hope denied.
Dense neutron stars inaugurate a secret space,
an operative form that a body might trace
in liquid intensity, and be never at home
to gold, copper, sacrificial blood, the metronome
the fortuitous alchemist sounds in his book.

3

1

Morning now appears, a green sari on a lake—
the actuality of it—a quantum field,
a biological satire always concealed
by coherence, revealed by the perfect mistake.

I would keep me where the garment goes, contrary
to my promises. All these small terms misconstrue
my prophesies, confound my syntax, and argue
that all contingent light becomes an adversary.

2

Who is the god of healing, if not Apollo?
And how can I erase my footsteps, if only
the gods know the path? Nothing has been bracingly
done; all here is provisional, a random flow.

If then love departs its orbit, what can be said
to figure art's resolve and measure, the chorus
dancing in Kọmọ's cradle, the ambiguous
design the aulós on its own seems to have bred?

3

Baca sets me an octave to encompass,
all affabile and agogic, a modest
suppression in its bones, even perhaps a jest
and figural inadequacy, a carcass.

You must remember that light remains Baca's prime
companion, a constant habit he devised
to embellish a fragile body, energized
by being coordinate, willful, and sublime.

4

I was never welcome at Alexandria,
with my bolí, my altars filled with jackal tails,
spices, carbon and precious metals, the details
that obscure the light and raise a nostalgia.

Aden could have taught me an efficient design,
a new translation and a doubling counterpoint,
perhaps a counterfactum and physical point,
a coherent scattering nothing could define.

5

So we might have spoken, if we could have, of death—
the awkwardness serving as testable statement,
youth's ingenuity only an adornment,
the impenetrable rhyme sounding faith and breath.

Hanoverians do their best to mimic
the poets by the river, those who would subvert
the electron's texture, the maladroit, covert
grace in which every magnitude remains caustic.

6

Such is the event, the primal necessity
engendered in the head that thinks the world, the word
that forms a radiance descending, an absurd
limit at once to substance and intensity.

Now, let all this suffice for one who will not dress
in love's disfigured garments, one who must remain
dissatisfied with eternity, or sustain
a fragile datum, a swift and blessed darkness.

Galileo perhaps believed that flowering pear
could match my dance,
                    an orbital extension
only the recently dead might fathom.
Nothing this high can live; everything flows
toward a ground state never fully entered.
                    So what will you have?
Here in Ajijic,
Diogenes will always awaken in this cranky fog,
and spread his fishnets, gathering
the beaded fish against his own apprehension.
He knows how to figure death's limitation;
therefore,
it does not surprise him that the Frenchman
has decomposed water,
and that air might take shape as breath, or wind,
or perhaps a god,
a body changing the signature of space.
Someone ought to uncover the burial ground
that animates this orchestrated sea,
and give in to that fragile music of forgetting,
go where all shadowy suspension is sign,
all abstract devastation embodied in the atom,

the indistinguishable rhythm that teaches patience.
You must remember the ohema,
the dirges she measured and numbered, and all
her songs relative to being.
                    Who could possibly
have captured that rhythm, taught its coordinates?
But you know that I am not, properly speaking,
an element,
defined by a koiné that seems to have lost its juice.
I am too unpredictable,
a star without an atmosphere,
yet I am always in search of that infinitely
                    perfect union.
What would my function be,
if there were no mathematical expression to tie me
to my confirmation?
                    Oh, such a misspelling,
a minor symmetry that binds me to my suffering,
perfect failures that persuade me that I am alive.
There you are again, my old friend, the Big Dipper,
with the two stars sitting tight in a cluster
                    that moves away from me.
All things move away from us.
So I will take my walk toward El Farol
and the tacos and beer that comfort me;
certainly, in that shade, I can contemplate
this Monday evening's promise, a boatride

through my own disappearance.

                        Never

let it be said that Galileo would constrain

such fulsome intuition, such fulsome attention

                to the perfect dance.

What can I do with this silence, the sovereignty
expressed in the cantankerous absence of mass
five? Whose clock now rhymes with that of the hummingbird,
engaged with bee balm, three bells gone, literati

of a summer afternoon? Forget that first word,
the Ovidian ratio that ought to pass
through the body's self-liberation, and then turn
through its own degradation. How extravagant

I have become, a mark on a printed page, such stern
evidence of structure, yet nothing consonant,
nothing given by a rule so inelegant.

Speak of the property of matter, the bright hand
that veils a water instance, the phenomenal
substance you see in the red mask, orchestral
balance that argues a transformative intent.
Plato, they tell us, found a system in the sand
around a wall, though every constituent
occasion recalled an absent measure, constraint
he could not abide or recall, the self-restraint
and melodic conversions he refused to hear.
I remember the morning office, the clergy,
whose gifts were paraphrase, sermons, and an ear
for an ecclesiastical asperity.
We were always companions, always sensitive
to the way we used numbers and formed the year.
Nothing could distress us, and the secular eye
the sun displayed appeared to our eyes subversive.

What does the initiate seek, if not
his own death? Think of this as the first day,
the sun upon the dolaba, the way
the dancers command the terrace and plot
the world's umbilical cord. That once shot

equation uncovers a disarray
in the spirit; one can dispute the play
the light proposes and the monoglot

irruption figured always in the mask.
Death, they say, sets all the numbers by hand.
Why call now upon the Damascene, grand

in suffering, with his transforming task
in place, his algebra only a bland
desire the initiate may not ask?

The Liatris has become Athenian,
a sacred grain, mark of a girl who dreams
perfection, the immutable extremes,
almost a strategy without a text.
What must the ascetic self, Marian
in its depths, understand by such a vexed
disposition of minor stars, canon
bound, all too discursive, all too common?
The infinite must endure unfolding,
or, as some might say, a blessed descent.
Think augury in premises, whirling
bodies ontologically content.
Qué muerte tan larga . . . you must forgive
the way I withhold my memory, string
my questions upon an air that seems bent
with an ambition that remains furtive.

Alfonso dreamed a melodic number,
a scriptural sound that would start his own
decline, and send him searching a region
of strophic ingenuity. Limber
ontology might speak in a somber

voice, being undone by parity's bone.
In this canonical world, form alone
becomes an invention to encumber

all substantive accounts of left and right.
There, certainly, the ground shifts to conceal
the structure and design that should appeal

to Alfonso's expressive gift and sleight-
of-hand; all intrinsic reversals seal
our preconceptions, make them watertight.

Trappists in Vina never read
the cumulus cloud, or give in
to the bush with the red temper
of sacrifice
in its clothes.

Element of element, red
optical intention, the spent
origin that grounds the perfect
fiber of light
the wood holds.

Picture the complementary
element, red clouds that always
mark a mountain's harmonic
inversion, new
conception.

One must read
the wild sorrel
in the bush, there where the impure
begin the rhythm of the dance,
the quiet undressing of cloud.

Summer is
a burning fruit,
the alumi plant's black presence.
The village has begun to move
toward limestone and sorrow's white heat.

To erase
the footsteps, think
of the resonant molecule,
time's structure in the soul, the light
that maps love's perfect measure.

What would you say of air that breathes, or lies
suspended in its braces? Could you reveal
that modifying sound, or the structure
that points us to a metabolic gift?

The poet here recommends her nature,
the abstract solution, the perfect seal
to this unfolding. The perfect cadence
teaches a contradiction, a fragile

embodiment or a limit grown dense
with an electron's resolve, all fertile
with displacement, improvised and tensile.

bọlọ sọ̃

Now that Alexandria has died
I would offer you a choice of stones—
     white limestone from Tura,
     the red and black granite out of Aswan,
     gneiss from the Nubian desert,
     basalt from El Faiyum,
     Egyptian alabaster from Tell el 'Amarna—
all the rocky solace that makes sitting at the tail
of Porto Alegre, above Buenos Aires, you might say,
                        tolerable.
I had carried you through Córdoba,
astonished by the banana leaves leaning
against a turquoise sky,
and even then had thought of the royal boats
near the valley temple,
and the weight of the pyramidal texts
        the river would disguise.
Everything the grave knew
had been covered in smoke, showered in incense.
The old families sat patching adobe,
filling wine skins with water to cool their parlors,
sitting in borrowed equipales,
having borrowed the bell to announce their funerals.

Be that as it may,

someone told me that Molinari had been arrested in San Blas,

betrayed by a hairshirt with a cannabis sweet tooth.

Believe it, Molinari es un gaucho.

No, sir, gauchos do not exist, only the ludic

Ludmer insists on their being.

We have this procession, taking possession of Hidalgo,

and then we will go skirting in Culiacán,

and perhaps take the ferry to La Paz,

to trade for that volcanic glass and touch

the sensitive spirit of the Cree.

Carolingian Trio

1

River deep as Pascal's abyss, Santa Fe ascends.
What could contradict us? Such a proposition
bleeds temper into truth, that first exposition
gathering death's danzón. No, no one here pretends

to have that Greek fable, the right disposition,
or desire the design elicits and expends
when the breath on its own, emerging, condescends
to abide, to divide a perfect intuition.

These hymns appear in spring, androgynous season,
and all the world withdraws to gather its reason.
All is concealed behind a spoken word, endless

evasion, unfolding nothing the eye can touch.
The Carolingian sang redemption with such
ferocity the Cusan found his anger seamless.

2

All winter cardinals compose flagellant
wings; impurity shades into an aberrant
purity, and the spirit wills
its own demise. Such a benediction defines
the Carolingian, never in tune with signs.
The poet alters his dunghills,

prepares his fall into a fit dislocation.
The Carolingian knows no confirmation
in flutes and altars, oxen adorned with graces.
These sentences leave no room for God's rehearsal,
no space for the attention to an orchestral
music only death embraces.

Even Paris has a volatile bird
sitting upon a gate, a most absurd
proposition someone might stitch
into an expansive singularity,
remarkable, ordinal, a density,
a performer with perfect pitch.

But who would ask a glass, to see his suffering,
or go fishing in the coldest night to bring
an elegiac warmth to bed?
The Parisian always claims he hears the cracked bell,
the voice in the fog, feels another's blood swell
beneath his skin. What could be bred

in that tempered body, what rhythm sound to trace
an absence *that* poet will propose, now as lace,
again as brimstone, or an echo
the Carolingian must thoroughly refuse?
Muso Koroni grew fat with nature's ruse,
her desire gone dry, the sotto

voce structure only an instant on a stream.
Molinari himself felt submerged in a dream,
perhaps that awkward companion
following ships. Wherever you begin,
you will read love's measure, the darkest origin,
a hymn to renunciation.

3

There must be a feathered brush for the day's ending,
        something that would tempt
that light from the plankton; certainly a cunning,
        though rather unkempt,

factum might surprise or go unnoticed, a sly
        notion to preempt
what never was at play. No one can tell you why
        water is exempt

when light circles its own darkness, or falls
        from figure to impulse
in the buried city. Nothing here forestalls

        that semantic pulse,
that repetitive, broken density,
        light's absurdity.

Homage to the Intrusive, Insubstantial, Hypertensive, and Insulting Ronald Firbank

1°

I live in Xico,
near to a cemetery which holds no one I know—
campesinos, licenciados, amas de casa,
trasnochadores, all the floral intelligences
                    that compose a village life.
I have followed the land's curve
away from a salutary pyramid, the smoke
that covers a wintry valley, to end here,
happily dancing in Xico's haze, content
with the Veracruzana day, lying briefly on its back,
cooling its body.
                    I could be pacified by tombs,
but none appears.
Yesterday,
I heard Langston singing his rivers.
He would place me on the Orinoco,
ever mysterious to his soul,
or on the Mississippi, where blood has formed

an indigenous house, mudstrong and unaccountable.
My anthropologist would have that affecting presence
embodied in the river,
or perhaps in the first structure that sits

                              on the Nile.
Nothing here accounts for my authority
over that round, sunbaked water bowl,
or over the bee that has captured a wasp.
                    I know that
                 a transparent solitude
                 measures juniper's
                        absolute form,
                        faithful in shadow.
This modulation,
a linear unfolding of soul into God,
gravity's modification, provokes a return
to a seething water, to Cernuda's boat,
         sitting upon its Brownian bottom,
all hallowed by mirrors, walls in the water,
nature's punning ambivalence,
              given substance in the Florentine's Paradise,
a black hole, germ and terminal, expansive
                        in its nothingness.
Well, now,
Chris is speaking Latin, better than that Greek anatomist,
or that impoverished Pole who kept his eye on a celestial
purity that had escaped the Greek.
                        Langston sits to argue

continuity with Guillén; they will ignore the graves in Xico,
and be solicitous of every accident and premise
that lacerates the skin of words.
Thunder has an itch to dance upon the terrace,
go softly with the cleansing of it;
yet something will always remain unspecifiable,
and the silly hat, the variable, will dance
                              in its own corner.
Still there is the obscure problem of matter and field,
a radial movement toward the center
                  even those in Göttingen find troublesome.
Xico remembers that cognate verb,
and the way the testaments sing, confronting
God with a familiar presence.
My arid buddy in Buenos Aires reads *his* Greek
by lamplight, courting a darkness in Democritus,
and the theology returning the world to its nothingness.
                  What will defend
against what will not, cannot, happen?
I remain a shady equilibrium,
possible only as disruption, an object of thought,
a series of one, and "one who will return from there."
Even so, I resist
the Scotian insistence that accident might be
a logical fault, a sin defined by nature's
                              catechism.
Have I told you about the trumpet solo that adorns
"Espelhos," a perfect displacement that tells us

all worlds alike end?

Count me a summoner,

though I would be an aguatero

      with a yoke upon his back.

You might find me attuned in Poza Rica,

the belles-lettres of fish mi orgullo in a dry town,

and, oh, by the spike of it, I will have a trental

in the plaza at Veracruz.

All here remains a spontaneous constitution,

though nothing appears after the art itself,

and there is only the matter of evaluating

       a proposition.

Daisy would know me.

But who but Molinari could teach Daisy Fawcett

the shape of the Rio Grande?

She will linger on her splintered porch,

under her patchwork quilt.

      Must Molinari

savor the ovaltine, bacon, beans and collards

she devises, and then become Jesuitical

about quilting in Propertius?

So we will keep our anguish in the vault.

Xico has a Malian impulse, a will

to explication, and thereby orders the change

       in its body.

I must have come home.

I will sit with this devastation of being,

this indifference to neglect.

2°

Macuta has become enigmatic,
and Peitho, standing near the open fire,
has turned impossible.
Nothing to be done.
                    The city must refuse its rest.
Kafka,
so says Stratis Thalassinos,
would never have understood Diana's presence on Reforma,
her sacred light devalued by the sacra.
Baca tells me I appear a pupil of melancholy,
a wrinkled child.
                    How does he know,
if I call myself Thomas, a Scottish divine,
in touch with contingency and science's perfect
sum of accident?
But, then, who listens to Firbank, or needs
to mark Macuta's rhythm?
Think on this endless, ideological conformity—
the radiant electron spiraling inward, falling,
its ambiguity responsible for a quarrel.
Even now, the Egyptian marks the shadow upon this body,

the tenuous state of all beginnings.
I came out of my mother's womb
a cosmic minstrel, already changing and moving.
I paid no attention to the Greek
                    who would have me think
                            of my real nature,
or of the effective passage from sense to mind.
Leave that to Thomas the Pythagorean Scot
                        and his broken line.
My text was never linear; you could hear such
fragmented density in the troubadour's melisma,
that detail of a body in crisis.
                        I urge you
never to winter in Buenos Aires,
where you might come upon an aura that speaks
of irrational invention,
                    and lose your way.
All here speaks negotiation,
though there is no place for negotiation,
when the tongue abandons the sacred,
and the sacred no longer feels un état spontané.
Our aesthetic tells us that Daisy must sit with her hymns
and become the ground for Baca's boleros.
            This mother is no lady.
And all music begins as a shape in harmonic space.

3°

Sit her in the king's seat, as still as death.
I wish I had another name for Daisy;
I would then obtain a macroscopic perspective,
and begin again the lyrical argument,
                                    an unfolding,
a modulation in the choir's intention,
and have no need for structures that conceal themselves.
Da capo,
I encounter the soul's arrival, with nothing
to prevent death's coming into being.
That first voice would have to be mistaken,
a significant variation only Cernuda
                                    would understand,
and Daisy would distinguish by scuppering doubt.
She knows the universe is subtle,
a breath rising from the depths, an *is*
that will not happen.
                                    Think of her ingenuity,
correcting Machaut, dealing gruffly with John the Scot.
You must discount that scandal in Corrales,
the coordinate system she had made from English

crystal, Colombian emeralds, quexquémetls from Oaxaca,
water jugs from Persia, everything a Sunday might embrace.
"Haec certa deserta
and Zephyr's air sits on the vacant grove."
Could it be, she says,
that the soul is not in a body
and that the Sandia Granite cannot keep a secret?
What can replace this revelatory language
that Daisy has learned to speak,
these confounding propositions, familiar recollections
of a force change?
Heraclitus has tried to redefine her ordinary existence,
reconfigure the order of her practical affairs.
He hears the silence in her attention to death,
and has followed her through a dry patch of summer,
looking for antelope horns, the inmortal
that echoes Asclepius.
She returns to this city,
for the economy of its presence, all
its limitless rules,
the moments she can weave in her gathering
and doing.
We had been in this garden before,
and had thought ourselves principled
by actual occasions,
the functional techné of a spider, too essential
to display a hidden grief.
Think of this all as a sensible motion,

downward,
                    searching a center.
The body circles this perfect silence,
Daisy's mathematical point.
We remain absolutely ready to agree
that eternity has a proper order,
and a voice that desert-bound evangelists
refuse to hear.
Nevertheless,
the Greek will direct us down this path
toward the real nature of goodness, a dialectic
that matches words with music, Daisy
                    with the Everywhere Now of death.
Time dances to the rhythm of another name,
evocative, evasive, syntactical.

Pauline Trio

1

One could sing October rain,
and one had a gift for plain
chant and prayer, a domain
unsettled by love or its
intimate other. What fits

with this theology no
one dares to say. These twins so
perfectly in tune must know
"the modesty of nature,"
the perfect art and texture

that sustains the other name.
Paris could not be the frame
for loyal Romans, their shame
worn upon their bodies light
as air, and nothing is quite

as endurable as death.
Those who have taken this path

move with an abiding breath.
Such a common dance this dense
intention of love's expense.

Keep this for that special hour
when the Roman drops his sour
gift for abandoned splendour;
et c'est la nuit, the footfall
that troubles that other Paul.

2

I have learned the felicity of fire,
how in its wake
something picks at buried seed.
Think this a most festive deed,
nature's mistake,
borrowed flare of a village dance, satire
of the sun's course, light you read
through waste, repair. Death had freed
that first opaque
habitation (what a widening gyre),
an aspen ache,
a lustrous scar that might lead
to a hidden grove, or breed
astonishment in its loss; all entire,
a shaping breath proposes its own pyre.

3

Solitude guides me
through this minor
occasion;
moon is my mentor,
one on a spree.
This notion,
night's philanthropy,
courts my favor.
Devotion,
love's predecessor,
sings its tidy
discretion.
Such gentility
reins all vigor,
all caution.

En una noche escura,
the Catalán considers his heritage.
What can he do with his desire?
Living day by day in Montréal,
he cannot think of wedding songs,
festival days in yellow fields;
he cannot dress in green.
"Hoy la vida morimos / en ajeno rincón."
Cernuda has taught him

      that silence is like this,
pleasures hidden in Tetuán.
Baca has given the Catalán

     a reason to escape.
   Schoolboy dreams,
   billetes,
   anillos,
   tales at a well-dressed table,
   transcendental arguments
   for a winter in Nova Scotia.
   I will not sing for a lover
   trimming a camisón with gold,
   working with silk,

smelling of sea salt and berries.
Who took the cloth from the cellar?
Who took the boy from the sea?
Leave me alone on a snowy bank
with my moon-touched lemon and lilies—
    "Quiero unicamente el viento de mi /
    país, llorándome."
Such is the merchandise of the Catalán.
What would he sell, if not unruly
benevolence, if not an anniversary
             with no season?

    I hold my life in a gold coin,
    with the face of one
    who counts me among his treasures.
    So the world appears,
    impersonal as suffering.
    The pun of existence pretends
    to limit my doubt;
    an improvised rhythm places
    me in nature's bath,
    offers a stringent immersion
    in love's cosmology.
What are the properties of substance?
Who is the Catalán?
Say that the soul moves, embraces all music,
the perfect paradox of sign and substance,

the pre-reflective mathematics of village solitude.

Say that I have become undone by the wedding blanket

I brought as a gift.

Nothing I have proposed

in the festival exigencies that have comforted me

is as valuable as stone,

or the river that marks this place as this world's

beginning.

A wedding song must begin

the first conception of all that is difficult

but true.

She sat, holding a match to an earwig,

all compassion and contemplation abruptly at hand.

Those who had known her father gathered themselves
in the doorway

and marveled at her instrumental ingenuity.

A vestry madness burdened the convocation.

Who would think that love could speak so solemnly

without provocation?

Could she arrange her spices and unguents,

and propel them into service before the banns,

when, haloed and trumpeted,

washed and cinched by a purple headscarf,

she would begin her memories?

Singing now:

> ¿Por que no viene, padre,
>
> por que no viene un día,
>
> que yo casarme quiero
>
> con el conde de Almería?

And yet I caught him by my will and ineffable longing,

and hold him secretly . . .

My body is various, infinite, and singular,

turbulent notions proposed by an exile.

I take this rhythm perdidamente

to the crossroads,
where all who would wound me
bring me their bands of cotton, eggs, and ashes.
I will speak with my father
                            about transcendence,
and offer him those moments which have no
                           authority or being.

sọ dayi

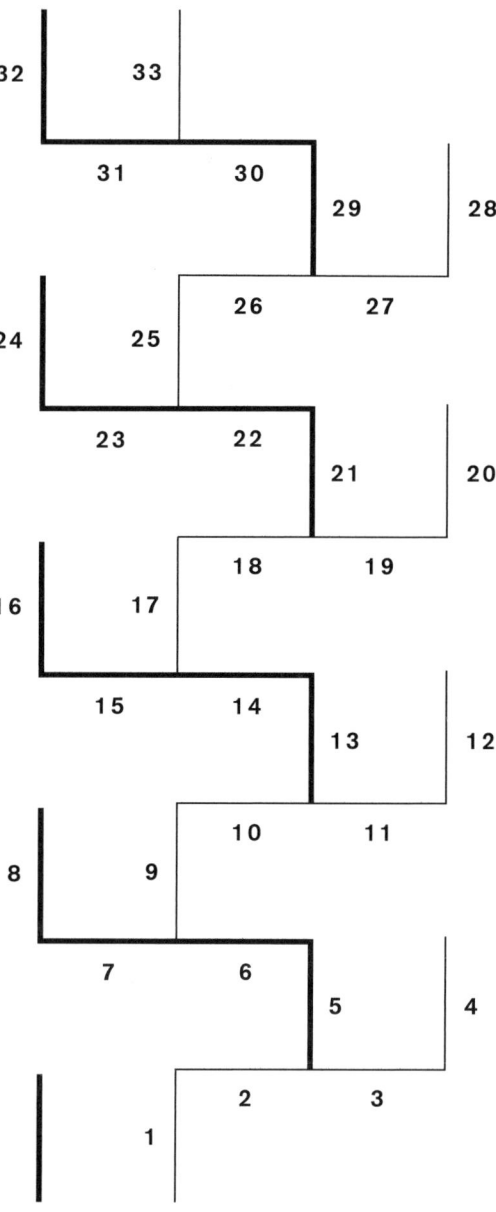

banã ngolo

Early winter
Eboussi-Boulaga waits
for the first
snow, the face
earth's cloud chamber will reveal.
Consider now
a shadow on this body,
how each small
essential unit becomes
a logical
constant, copula that will
have nothing
to do with existence, no
life-bearing
form.

32   33

1

There remain modifications
to my dance, prefigurations
embodied in loom and kapok tree, service
and force, tenseless and free.

All that is here agile and bound resists,
insists upon its ground
of silence, a parallel stance
that scale and key only enhance.
Oh, quanta dolorosa bellezza!

×

Romanos has a silver hymn
to his soul, its strict shape as trim
as Russell's metrical triad, symbol
nimble enough—ironclad.

The third becomes a fiction, concrete,
fleet, a contradiction
often justified yet defied
by order never clarified.
Who could be insensitive to tumult?

31   30

Does Archytas mean this broken line,
the initiate's angled design,
everything that fell from purity?
He has no faith in a lunar month,
no mathematics for a child's birth,
no independent form contrary
to its promise, a song's argument
with its maker. He cannot invent
an order's disposition and depth.

✗

Why tax the Scot with experience,
generation's end, subservience
to a parallel order, the breath
that modifies this disclosure space?
Every proposition will retrace
itself; all melodies court a death.
Archytas might never recognize
this mountain's roots, the magma's disguise,
that silent, harmonic interval.

26   27

Molinari sits, per affectum displaced,
on the Orinoco, disdainful of Greek
inflections, diminished intervals—disgraced
by his own fragility, an incomplete
capacity for spatial forms, the concrete
unfolding of a red stone, caustic, debased.
Saya might soon reveal his soul's oblique
mathematics as an act of will, embraced
by apostrophe, benevolent exchange.

✗

An electron is an aural presence upon
this river, so say the bell and altar
changing its disposition, the eidolon
of sacrifice, a tyẹ bóló disguised
as female, left-handed, numbers compromised.
Molinari will propose a lexicon
of limits, and read again the secular
aspiration of katharmoi, the withdrawn
reciprocal of Athens, the broken line.

23   22

If each element has its value,
what now could guarantee the immutable light?
The poet chambered beneath the earth
searches light's shadow/nothing is relatively benign
                    nothing is dangerous → nafolo
must follow the experimental closure sebaya brings /
consider this qualitative progression (whatever may be
an object of thought, a term without concept,
                        accountable assertion).

    ×

Find me a synonym for rupture,
the discontinuous macroscopic perspective,
the point of one, or one, ἔστι, the duge
given substance by a liminal figure.
That, within this chamber, speaks to a troubadour's
melisma, a structural crisis invented
                    by a curved orbit.
This relation becomes an ensemble of the dead,
no place for negotiation.

1 8   **1 9**

Having no syntax, the Greek must rely
upon solitude and disenchantment
with a lady, a perfect amendment
found in light's sorcery and secrecy.
The soul, an abyss within a sphere, learns
what altars express in carbon and gold,
a severed hand, a detached eye, a scaffold
resting on a singular foot, the urns,
with whirlwind and sign, fixed, immutable.

×

The permissible electron traces
a contradiction; Xico disappears;
I live eternity's distance with ears
attuned to a buried horn that laces
this design to the initiate's fall.
Such misapprehension soon imposes
the liberated self, the direction
of the double, Binu's indiscretion,
the embellished field that soon closes.

15   14

Baca has learned (just
                of brook
the musical form—
                Petrus
        tells us Baca finds
        solace:
                        archaic plainsong
                        aulós
                        Hamiltonian
                                nurtured
                        nurturing bolí:
music
bodied in Kọmọ's
force field /
                Petrus at this point
sings time's
arrival upon
                itself (

Daisy's number becomes an axiomatic
function, an ordinal guide for her existence;
this, order tells that root, braving Heraclitus
and milkweed, Mujynya's fragile and emphatic
place, the one resolute Lagrangian substance
of old music and insensible invention.
Call it an mnemonic device, intention
that grows in campo aperto acutely grave,
the harmonies constrained by a receding wave.

✖

At this hour, Thalassinos wades through his glacial
memory of the sea, all that russet color
of absent astilbe. Such consequential
amplitudes foreshadow a curled demeanor
Stratis would soon impose upon a solar flare,
an untranslatable event, burdensome, spare.
Who now will focus upon that reversible
compound, the hemisphere another frame prior
to the body's proposition, abstract, unstressed?

7   6

You know that there exists an object,
an event that will not come forth,
a superimposition that shadows itself,
and now compels the Scot to affirm
that number is a truth beyond
"external jurisdiction"—conceive, if you dare;

or dare the cut, thought's bright incision
set within elements that frame
no economy of signs, no ordinal domain.

×

Baca knows density, a white escape,
a sun compromised by an axiom of separation,
an indiscernible Leibniz; he argues
with a Kintu disposition that ascends and descends,
an impossible order that will shape
his soul's order and will guide his introspection.
Why should Baca display his soul's virtues,
the alphabet and melody that nothing here amends?
Whose is this life-bearing form?

2   3

Love will go unnoticed, or will become
the first language, a frightful beginning for bodies
fit only for ambiguity,

                       a cadenced movement
becoming a dance, a perfect origin that sits
apart from its own construction.
Who will reason now
with the pace of our embodiment
and a legacy that proposes the bone's
irresolvable archive?
I have been instructed to forget

                       an inauthentic birth,
and compelled to see in the resonant light
a binding of bodies that will not move,
or cannot be compelled to move, toward their death.
What is the quarrel,
the metrical proposition that will not admit
a beginning, will not sustain a symmetry?

The body here contradicts its own dogma.
There is that moment when biblical Baca,
having scratched and bottled the Chimayo air,
stands at the end of the road that leads to the river,

a geistige force justified by being nothing at all,
and renews the river's name.
The river's gravity will become our signature,
sign upon sign,
that only a calculus designed at Paris might uncover.

This Albuquerque morning begins its hostile intervention,
a dyadic relation without a subject or proposition.
Baca pretends that he has chosen my frame,
and tells me he has conceived an imperishable element
as a gift.
                    But I know there is an end to physics,
and a shading of languages
that can only become a logos of logos,
or the perturbation in an atom absorbing light.
The German tells us these qualities are derivative,
as furtively endowed as Kọmọ's cradle.
Let me take my reflection from fire,
the possible mark upon this place, this face
that will become the first thought

                                   in the shadowed world.
That initial authority,
spiraling upon itself, might also contradict

                                              itself.
Writing always goes against the grain.
Someone has said we come into the world
already dispossessed,
a contradiction of that mother force,

a challenge to that first flash, a spiral
moving inward, leading me to think
beyond my possession.
I have heard that only the hunters know the words,
only the very old can speak with assurance.
Why now begin this instrumental focus,
such a burden of material being,
or the mathematical assumption, a rhythm
in every term's definition,
when every proposition denied might be
                              true, or false?

Baca knows my narrative,
the gauge symmetry
encompassed by my duge stone.
He has found me near the river,
sketching a watery figure with a forked stick.
I had, I thought,
become a kouros, a structured hesitation,
a dimensionless copula, complete,
a self-presenting mode.
The Dane was busy, at that moment,
with my circumstance, the linguistic virtue
of all probable and provocative event.
I had my Ecuatoriano in stitches
with my tales of the Egyptian, ferrying Greeks
toward the navel of the world.

You will believe such darkness distributed
                    with such exhilaration.
Baca knows I have proposed my own double,
rising from the ensemble of the dead,
one who is justified in a discontinuous
                           silence.
Certainly, counting is irrelevant,
and the electron's superfluous journey
to its assignation
                    sets the quarrel
near a burial ground, and figures
that discoverable third who sits now veiled.
Why tax Baca with proof?
Why install him near creation's disruption,
and ask for the blistering qualities of belief?

Love, we say, is a relational composition,
a fortuitous and reversible compound,
nel qual si questi l'Animo, and yet
nothing satisfies. Some say
I have drawn dolaba into this decay,
and have removed my body from its
singular history,
thinking my every act an inventory
of disrupted passion, a resolution that structures
a tangible constellation.
                    Speak now of the one

who will return to this hemisphere,
to that power of occasion, the estate that grows
                    from impurity.
Should we be dressed now for a sacred entrance, or
for the probable and corrigible dimension
the electron knows?
                    All there is opposition;
there is nothing in that liminal state
that breathes nature's content,
or the supplemental completeness that makes
that final word an affective psalm.

Follow my language
through this sacred chain:
sesame
serpent mask
albarga
calabash
neutron
proton
singularity.
All is superposition,
an epistemic notion, a rhythm,
all, number and measure relative to substance.

I should invite Baca to my choir,
make him a patron of Kọmọ,

but I hear him tapping far below the earth
in search of an unseizable microstate
                    he insists on calling his soul.
What does he know of the sun,
its radiative zone, its convection?
And why should he believe in enduring
                                configurations?
Perhaps it would be better to number my presence,
and to feel the changing shape that takes me away from,
and into, myself. Perhaps it would be better
to acknowledge a star-fed music
                    that will not sound.

Three a.m.
I awaken to the Little Bear.
The alchemists in Cambridge are measuring
the distance between Polaris and my yellow birch.
I see there "that trace of darkness that cannot be recalled,"
in the proscriptive adobe altar,
turning around my own fallibility,
                    a fundamental descriptive spin,
where the domain goes blind.
Help me to recall another darkness—
my father, waking at three a.m. in Madrid,
prepared to affirm the reality of sheep, or to invent
the epistemology of wine,
"the clearing-concealing advent of being."

Love, we say, is an ordinal experience,
comprehensive,

           a birthday and anniversary,
a word's reason for being.
Baca senses a conspiracy,
a possible rupture, an altered alphabet.
And yet he and I know
that all is melody,
a proposition of acceptable silence,
the visible limit of a body,

           clarified, justified,
one that has disappeared.

The Sonata's Moral Grammar

A

PRIMA

Molinari feels light's concealment,
knows the paradox in glã, the wind
under just that first authority.
He recalls the furry insistent
galaxy that knows itself divine.

That first rational cutting confounds
two bodies so calm in their clarity,
giving place to an insatiable
double event.

SECONDA

What can descend if fire is moving water,
death's apparition, plenitude's revolt,
nafolo's planetary theater?

I say I am the mouth of the beast, the red
critical movement, spiraling inward;

it would be better to become instrumental,
the omniscient bird's learned companion,
a millet stalk that rests on a quill,
here, where all bodies appear primordial.

B

Malinke words no longer appear ascendant
authority in the mother. Elements turn
within that excision, a qualitative change,
a standing away; listening for pity's sound,
that intangible form—khu/kopf—an inversion
that scales a new modulation, finds no strange
co-extensive being and nothing to concern
that optimal stability or the sign spent
by its fragile measure, or its bound intention.

Mako is a Dedekind cut, a visible
intention of faith's dispersion, the abstract form
of that first voice—kómá, kũ, keleña, all death's
secret power. The body knows simplicity,
how to speak ages without a word structured by
death, and so we know ourselves incomplete, breath's
undulating syntactical limit, a swarm
of probable constellations, nothing sensible,
a grammar lost, a law of devastated stars.

A

The mother cuts the light from head to tail, rubs it
with hyssop; remains faithful to truth's event,
the consequence of small metaphysical words.

This speaks disarray, a masculine integer
that has found no place and no transformative tree,
only perhaps a limit to being, a process
measurable by absence, an adjectival
proposition composed by that first empty duration.
Could these intuitive intervals structure bone,
or a cellular improvisation arise
when the eye sounds its A? In campo aperto,
solitude counters spirit's light and becoming.

×

Some will say that first light has no properties
on its own, that space wears only a bird's plumage,
that the east betrays only its impurity.

This logician has lost faith in moving waters,
in the asylum of hemispheric altars.

But the mother knows that otherness, the rhythmic
descent into reflection and the apparent
density of a scattered seed and the image
of grain on the altar, knows the deformation
of a sign without a name, the body without
its stellar burial, the logos without its
absolute zero, its masked and burning orí.

CODA

A solar flare begins its oscillating dance,
a spiraling contradiction of gravity
and time; the mask sets its cross-examination
of number free from "external jurisdiction."
The dead in Mali tell us that we must embrace
imperfection, the silence at the root of truth,
coherent ambiguity, light's inversion.
What do we say when the fire descends in a cold
season, a woven band, refusing to be composed?